WAR
&
Pieces

WAR & Pieces

Dirk D. GRIFFIN

Per Bastet

War & Pieces

Copyright © 2019 Dirk D. Griffin

ALL RIGHTS RESERVED

No part of this book may be reproduced or transmitted in any form or by any means, electronic or mechanical, including photocopying, recording, or by any information storage or retrieval system, without prior written permission from the copyright owner unless such copying is expressly permitted by federal copyright law. The publisher is not authorized to grant permission for further uses of copyrighted selections printed in this book. Permission must be obtained from the individual copyright owners identified herein. Requests for permission should be addressed to the publisher.

Published by Per Bastet Publications LLC, P.O. Box 3023 Corydon, IN 47112

Cover art by Dirk D. Griffin

ISBN 978-1-942166-56-6

For readers, dreamers, and lovers

Special thanks to my friends who continue
to encourage my writing

WAR
&
Pieces

CONTENTS

Travelogue 1
    I. Beyond 3
    II. Compass 4
    III. Measuring 5
    IV. Passage 6
    V. Propinquity 7

Journeys 9
    Expectations 11
    Forward 12
    The Traveler 13
    Flight 14
    Hejira 15
    Where Flows the Soul 16
    Separation 17
    Busted Blues 18

War 19
    Boys Unripened Yet 21
    La Belle Dame Mon Seul Regret 24
    At the Door 27
    Witness 28
    Traum der neuen Welten Mein Engel 29
    In That Winter Country 30
    Vision of the Omega 31
    Before Swine 32

Love 33

Striding 35
Blue 36
Coyote 37
Beside 38
Absalom 39
Remainder 40
Muse 42
He Speaks 44
Two AM 45
Harry's Blue Rock Blues 46
Fire and Ice 47
Sunset 48
Dark of the Moon 49
Lonely is the Night 50
Taken 52
You Can't 54
A Haunting 55

Moments 57

And Morning Came 59
Land of the Broken 60
Poet in a Hat 62
City 64
Crazy Old Man 65
I Am Told 66
Jimmy Bailey 67
Isaac Remembers 69

Natural Beauty 70
Prière du Matin Pour les Morts 71
Shadows 73
Come Spring 74
How To Save Yourself 75
Like Pollock 77
Night Cat 78
Sometimes Art 79

Dreaming 81

Visit 83
Sweet Swing 84
Without 85
Ash 86
Designer Genes 88
The Scrying Pool 89
A Dream of Happy Cows 90
River Ghosts 92
My Song 94
Fellini 95
Slaking 96
Transformation 97
Dream Echoes 98
Stillborn 99
Vespers 100
Burning Faith 101
Mersey Beating 102
The Offer 103
Flash Photography 104

The Sacred Arts Quartet 105
    I. Geometry 107
    II. Music 108
    III. Numbers 110
    IV. Cosmology 112

About the Author 115

Images

All Images by Dirk D. Griffin

Vanishing Point 1
Berlin Wall Detail 2
Navigation 9
Blessed Isolation 10
War 19
Waiting To Fall 23
Love 33
The Way Down 34
Angry Sky 51
Winner 57
Village Idiot 61
Crooked Sky 81
Brandenburg Gate 87
River Ghost 93
The Sacred Arts 105
Floating Universe 109

TRAVELOGUE

Berlin Wall Detail

I. Beyond

there is a wall that calls to me
speaks my name
whispers desire
rises grey above my horizon

it haunts me
and never gives
simple answers
taunts me
when i ask for reasons

there is a wall that pushes me
holds me here
burns me to ashes
leaves me with questions

there is a wall that takes my voice
that takes my heart
that takes my truth
promises me everything

there is a wall that is my love
all i know
all i feel

all and all and all

there is a wall

II. Compass

a curious thing the compass
it knows the truth of North
and North is a good truth to know

but in speaking that wintery truth
what does it tell tell us of West
of deserts or oceans
of sunsets or twilight

and can it sing of South
a tune with warmer sounds
a wave of tropic heat
sand upon a beach

does it know the truth of East
can it feel the rising warmth
mornings yet to come
horizons filled with dawn

spinning through the points
North to West
South to East
but its only promise
spinning through
North it seeks
for North is true

III. Measuring

distance
how long the distance
what promise
what love
what anger
what fear
what can i wish this instance

the distance measures me
and takes what i can not keep
it falls away clutching at my collar
pulling me across the distance i imagined
pulling me through the distance

distance
who can call beyond it
coming darkness
seeking comfort
losing nothing
giving promise
perhaps in truth unfit

the distance measures me
and takes what i can not keep
it falls away
it falls away
distant

IV. Passage

crossing the fevered desert
sun in the distance
time at my back
i exist
i am now
i am then
i am yet to be

among the nothingness
skimming the black ribbon
each moment falls away
at once waking
i am now
i am then
i am yet to be

a shell of steel
a shell of flesh
an essence
scrambling forward
i am now
i am then
i am yet to be

V. Propinquity

a thousand miles can
change everything
perception altered
distance lost
distance made
perspective found

a thousandth of an inch
can change everything
between beside
a wisp of hair
a warm breath
a brush of lips

there you are
thinking of the thousandth mile. . .
and the closest touch
where you are

eyes closed
miles fall away
chasms close
your heart travels
your mind wanders
a thousand miles
a brush of closeness

where you are
thinking of the closest touch. . .
and the thousandth mile
there you are

JOURNEYS

"Come dress yourself in love, let the journey begin"
~Francesca da Rimini~

Blessed Isolation

Expectations

preparations have been made
screens on windows
doors locked
drinks on the porch
rocking gently
in the glider
while sun and moon
divide the last of
blue from the sky.

all preparations made:
shift back and forth,
i am never ready for dusk,
nor to lay down in the night.
yet here it is:
i listen, eyes closed,
chilled dew covering me.
in silent repose

Forward

ticket bought
all but ten dollars
to take me
somewhere

i forget the
destination

unimportant

once there the
journey

begins

The Traveler

once
walking into an
unknown town
i went down

suckerpunched

lying in the dust
of that
infrequently
traveled road
warm, red
blood flowing
from my nose
over my split
swollen lip

my eyes from
darkness to haze
to clarity
saw that
which lost
moments before
went unobserved

ironwork arch
dark against the sky
stretched from side to
side of that path
written in archaic
letters the twisted
ferric script called out

"Welcome to Bliss"

Flight

freely fly the crows
to the orange-red horizon
a single black cloud
i trudge along this dirt path
and struggle to reach the sunset

the sun is fading
my mouth left dry from the dust
and still the crows fly

a cacophony
their wings beat on loud and strong
they will reach their goal
my weakness now forces me
to rest beneath a willow

the sun slips away
and in the night i find rest

Dirk D. GRIFFIN

Hejira

the dust of forgotten trails
rises with my passing:
faith the journey
and love the destination
among, within this dry heat desire

and i know the call is singing
bringing truth to haunt my steps
who could follow me
into this wilderness

the dust is my companion
tells of holy days
when others walked where
i now follow amid the
thick heat's rise

i hear the call still singing

this sacred journey takes me
to places now unknown
from borders never written
to borders long past gone

i hear the journey calling
i feel the destination
i touch the call still ringing
i am the heat still rising
into the sacred night

Where Flows the Soul

rocking as the river
rolls calling to my
ancient soul

my spirit rises
wet for travel
and flows—

plunges deep
beneath the currents

breaks surface
turns down again
moving through depths
moving beyond
this frozen moment

here the river is all

we rush
toward the great
ocean

strive to touch
distant shores
united

Dirk D. GRIFFIN

Separation

water—

discarded

poured out
into a stream

joins the rushing
currents swept
away through the night

—wants only

the pail

Busted Blues

busted and broken and on the run
busted and broken i'm on the run
i never knew love could hurt someone

walking down a time-lost road
wandering down that time-lost road
carrying memories a heavy load

and the sun sets angry in the west
angry he falls orange in the west
i didn't give all, but i gave my best

so tomorrow when your morning dawns
when you wake tomorrow to your morning dawn
know i took my sorrow and just moved on
lonesome and hollow i just moved on

WAR

"Mankind must put an end to war before war puts an end to mankind.
~John F. Kennedy~

Boys Unripened Yet

boys unripened yet growing
in the blistering brilliant sun
of a red-stained summer

each experience in life
each experience in death
accompanied by shrill shouts
of unaccustomed words

they know nothing of land
or claims of ownership
exchanging fiery volleys
in terror and indifference

what will bring them to manhood
but the pale promise of violence
brazen in doorways and windows
offering her costly high
for free to those who will
share her carnal orgy
of disease and destruction

images jumble and memories lie
nothing is what it seems
and it seems nothing
a casual kill commonplace
a bloody stump
charred playthings
among the dead

this is how we raise them
with a bowlful of bullets
camouflaged comforts
and the song of rockets
lingering in an echo
of twilight's final flash

Dirk D. GRIFFIN

Waiting To Fall

La Belle Dame Mon Seul Regret[1]

i am in New York
could be London
or Paris
or any city alive
with the noisy
stench of decadence

unnoticed
at a small
sidewalk café
i sit among my silent
prayers
drinking water
eating hummus

disturbed by a rose
growing broken from
a pale hand

"God loves you"

i look, she is perhaps twenty
soft, scented sweet

"God loves you,"
she says,
"Don't be sad,
He has a plan for
your life."

i notice her eyes
lovely and green
her lips like the rose
skin bright clean

Dirk D. Griffin

she wears her
beauty like summer wears
sunlight
how can she
not know herself a harlot

she is temptation
i will not have

i take the flower
pricked by the thorn
mumble through
her apology
that it is all right
that yes
there is a plan

her eyes swallow me
i hear the click
it is come

this café is the mortar
and i the pestle will
grind out holy retribution

many sounds
mix with the
agonies of terror
pain fills and
fulfills me

i bloom fire and steel
a flower of divine
anger a roar to
smite the
unworthy

i could be in Paris
red lips near mine
perfume whispering
unholy acts in my head
emerald eyes my world

At the Door

paces from the open door
beneath a crying sky
a blaring sound
breaks and bellows

a bright blast blossoms
another petal crowns the
tenebrous flower of war

from this orchid
bloom of anguish
pours forth the bitter
nectar strength

intangible hope
now remains distant
unnatural as
honey from a rock

it is here the wayward
bride destruction
mutters death and pain
mutters angry in the chill
of a pounding rain

Witness

shelter in the blackness of the night
falling between two buildings
white fear fills my eyes
still the thunder echoes
still my heart pounds
still the night goes on

i pray
blindness save me from
the savagery of their wrath

thunder and another life
drains red onto the grey concrete

i pray
silence falls
between the echoes

thunder and again the dull thud
of emptiness smacks the earth

i pray
each breath
that night might
swallow me

thunder
i pray
leave me
witness

Dirk D. GRIFFIN

Traum der neuen Welten Mein Engel[1]

morning light
spills random through the alleys
and another day's meals
are picked from
other lives
discarded

dispossessed
you search
for mother
or father

tatterdemalion
mucous framing
swollen lips
dirt crusts your eyes
wandering

who has brought you here

what angel lies beneath
clothing stained torn
what language finds your voice

when the night covers you
shadow-sheltered in some
peeling boarded doorway

what worlds do you dream

---

[1] Dream of new worlds my angel

In That Winter Country

it was in that winter country,
where the cold would kiss
and bloom rich reds
on his cheek
he first heard them crying
in the white, barren
hillsides: where spirits
shuffle and shrug
in indifferent postures.

it was in that barren valley
when the jackdaw caws his
raven mistress to feast
on frigid forgotten limbs
broken in the valley
freshly spread with snow

it was beneath his shield,
beneath his tabard where he last
saw the dark of sky frown down
his sword, shattered by his side;
labored breaths jerked his body,
he ached for the life pouring in clouds,
dissipating before his fading sight.

it was in that winter country,
with the waning of the light;
that he knew, he understood,
with the clarity loss brings.
that spirits speak in whispers
and ravens gather grim,
wanting gives to needing
and needing is lost to men.

Dirk D. GRIFFIN

Vision of the Omega

i am the emptiness
of the world

my softest steps echo
in the desolation

of spirit of flesh
of companionship

i am the last among
the fallen

withered leaves at my feet
the world broken
and lost
by my command

Before Swine

pearls fall
the fragile thread broken
they cascade
down through
thick air

slowly
each perfect
white ball
flees to
individual orbits
evades capture
hits cold
marble

bounces again
and again
away from you
away from me

each separate
sphere seeks
its own orbit
beyond us

LOVE

"We are born of love; love is our mother."
~Rumi~

The Way Down

Striding

i stride
into darkness
hazy rain misting

through overcast
i suck oxygen
wetness expelling
carbon in exchange
for breath

a lover's kiss

striding each step
more purposeful
each movement
torching muscle

the light creeps in
forward, forward
the day begins

the sun ascends steaming
the wayward rain
i stride onward
in risen glory
still wet with passion

Blue

each spring i am called to
the blue

my paddle and kayak
ready to wander miles
of alternately rough
and gentle water

i think always
of you
your eyes wide with
joy sliding from boat
to rushing waters
you would laugh and splash
breaking the surface

those days were true
when i smile
it is for me
it is for you
riding our pleasures
upon the blue

Coyote

how you tricked
me laughing
at my loss

you promised
but lied in the
same words

and still i believe
you can be trusted

even though
tricks are your trade

Beside

the deep orange sun
falls behind the world
shadows gather reaching
toward me

alone beside my tears

the evening chill embraces
dew on my skin
no one here
to comfort

alone beside my tears

the sun arises
warming the earth
burns away fog
still I am here

alone beside my tears

Absalom

black locks
curling down
below your
shoulders
thick with
promise
perfumed by oils
matched by the
depths of
your dark eyes

speak to me
in the sweet
voice that
turns desire
to you

seduce me with
your eyes with
sweet breath with
words of beauty

caress me with
your olive skin
scented shining

breathe on me
your lies
and I will lie
with you
knowing betrayal
is your only love

Remainder

you left in morning light
determined to shake the dust
of our lives and scatter it
upon a rushing wind

i failed to speak—
why complain—
what could i say
without sounding childish
what words could equal
the imagined abyss of
a life separate from you

memory
that sad
fedora found while
thrifting at the salvation
army store

returned
later to the bin
no longer suiting you
left for others to pick over
kind and unkind alike

i fail this test
my heart hasn't the
muscle to keep
beating under
this weight
this heat of passion
fired by you
has left it liquescent

Dirk D. GRIFFIN

molten memories
dissolve collapsing
into a caldera
seething for release
left in morning light
crying out for peace

Muse

your whispered visions
surged through me
gave strength
made pain
endurable
and loss
less bitter

but they were yours

without them
i am lost to time
my heart shrinks
and my days grey

i await your return
knowing someday
visions will give
me life to share
and hope
to love

for want of you
among artifacts of my past
there was a small brown
unremarkable box

it contained letters of love
exchanged through passions
and the distance that separated
our souls

in a time when the moon
sailed sacred and the stars
were conspiratorial companions
to the desires and fires
of youth

and now grown grey
such words launched
from the page forcing
memory to life
to waking dreams
of how we were born
and lived
and separated

crushed flowers
clichéd phrases
want
need
loss

expectations and desire
wore against you

and you fled
leaving me
an unwilling island
with only
this box of you

He Speaks

he speaks to me
words sweet
dangerous
breath heavy
with absinthe

invited
harm will come
destruction flow
worlds will end
with love

his warmth washes
me with each syllable
focus lost

i am his

he speaks to me
blind i follow
giving myself over

Two AM

behind the counter
a coffee machine
spits its last few drops
into a fresh pot

even near the stove
there is a two am
early winter chill
crawling up my back
as i wait for breakfast
a fresh cup and you

we are traveling between
lives: our old ones gone
where we can't return
our future somewhere else

right here
right now
only love sustains us
untested we followed that
love in faith that now seems
tired, worn as the vinyl of these
ancient booths

we are travelers
in a country without maps
moving through the neon
night toward an unknown
dawn

Harry's Blue Rock Blues

friday night belongs to the lonely
harry plays his aging upright only
when the night has come
'round midnight when the night has come
to kiss his tears
to voice his fears

here in Blue Rock when the moon shines out bright
everyone whispers 'bout harry's lost sight
whispers in gossip
'gainst commandments they gossip
about his life
oh, his life and wife

harry drinks whiskey, bangs black and white keys
music swells up, oh it begs and it pleads
where is my jenny?
his voice gravels in, where is my Jenny?
long gone away
without words away

harry macrae is left moaning these blues
In his poor little room with rot-gut for booze
when loss is too much
lord without mercy when loss is too much
and pain always follows
oh pain always follows
pain

Dirk D. GRIFFIN

Fire and Ice

my words ice and shatter
to a broken gypsy melody
each portion
ground to wet slush
beneath a drunken waltz

there is no memory
complete enough to hold
the simple
angry
facts
you threw
at the slivered moon

i seek the warmth
that knowledge may impart
and shiver in the dark

Sunset

in the orange-red distance

blackbirds crawl
horizon-ward

in long summer shadows

children argue
over nothing

in my shaking hand

a half-eaten peach
drools slowly

in this absence

they are all
somehow
you

Dirk D. GRIFFIN

Dark of the Moon

this new
moon night

little light

the hues
of blue

dim

distant

somewhere
chanting

somewhere

you

Lonely is the Night

earth alone
turning traveling
beside its single
moon knows
the darkness
miles beyond
the sun

and the moon
hidden from
our star's
warmth far
forgotten
from its
fiery stare

shadows slink
around the
blue
how lonely
is the night
eclipsed
i wait for
you

Angry Sky

Taken

war in destruction
cut down love and uprooted
hope
deadly words were aimed to kill

the touch of pestilence
withered all beauty
weakened it to despair

famine kept
companionship distant
friendship hungry
loyalty sparse
lost in depression and darkness

death severed the few remaining
bonds that desperately held
a crumbling life built
through adversity
through hardships that proved
love can survive almost
anything

the horsemen have come
i see you in the arms of war
without a backward glance
where are your
vows and covenants
against just such a loss

Dirk D. GRIFFIN

death rides on and waves
the spare threads of our life
worn thin by pestilence
tattered by famine

waves them in victory
at a dying yellow sky

You Can't

you can't break me
with beauty
beauty has betrayed
my trust

you can't break me
with amusements
for all my entertainment
falls to dust

you can't break me
with sun or shade
or love or pain
you can't break the one
whose life is
unjust

A Haunting

you alive
in setting sun
colors fade
to dark blue

i alone—
you undone—
left in shade
to wonder

still
i am all
that's left

all that's left

among these ghosts of leaving

MOMENTS

"Miracles come in moments."
Wayne Dyer

Dirk D. GRIFFIN

And Morning Came

oh, how red the morning
lips that kissed the new
day's greying hillside
how it whispered
how it muttered
on a porch men cried
for the loss of night
singing memories in choked
tones dying with the light.

Land of the Broken

in the land of the broken
photographs are fading
in stacks

chemicals consume
the past
you watch eyes
dimming

eucalyptus, menthol, and
captain jack hang on each scented
altar

broken mirrors in corners
belie the truth believing can't
be seen

steel cuts cold and icy leaving
red flowing into the white
foaming

here are all the battles won
lost, drawn, breathing in
rhythm

here is the last stand
the kingdom of the broken
voiceless

Village Idiot

Poet in a Hat
For Rob

his words quietly
wind up scales to the ninth
and down again
diminishing the fifth
skipping past four to
a bluesy third
they tumblefall
ignite senses
imagespark
satiating the ear
while stomach
growls

stumblewalking
down bright
streets
he lifts his face
full in the sun
bright with words
like music
like laughter
like sorrow
like morning
and you know
as chorus
words fall to
your hand
in verse without
measure

Dirk D. GRIFFIN

head lowers
still singing
his face slightly shadowed
though moving in light
watch in stunned silence
words filling your mind
in this way and that
verses still echo
from the poet in a hat

City

i am lost
this city
surrounds me
confuses me

how can you
be so alone
in such a sea
of people?

i drown in the
volume of humanity
pulsing around me

strangers press me
i swim alone

Dirk D. GRIFFIN

Crazy Old Man

bent from keying
code into the
ever-hungry
maw of needful
binary dreams

greying and grim
wrapped in clicks
never-hearing
shouts of living
beyond senses

simply thinking
without feeling
something settles
vague upon him
dimly calling

eyes are failing
darkened edge
translucent views
light receding
to where we lose

I Am Told

i am told that bears in hibernation
can still be roused to anger when disturbed
and sleeping dogs are better often left
to lie and while the harmless hours by
but I could never mind such sane advice
when faced with bald and callous thoughtless acts
pushed on undeserving hapless victims
by giants taking more than any share.
those wasting all that others might require
to simply live and make their life each day
they surfeit greed through sacrifice of those
thought lacking an exalted state of grace
in this i find i must provoke the bear.
i must the dreaming dog from stupor wake
to take the burden from a world that aches

Dirk D. GRIFFIN

Jimmy Bailey

i dreamed of travel
foreign worlds
exotica called
my name

visions of wildly colored
flowers and songs in
unknown languages
filled my senses

sunlit beaches
burly cities
love and adventure captured
my soul; i planned
all of that
all of that
all of that
and more

now i travel destinations
between two points
assisting other travelers
some always the same
some never to be seen again

working the train
is traveling without
going anywhere
a treadmill of sameness
on the move

there are no beaches
washed in sunlight
and no surf pounding
in the night

between and at each end
i am always here

Dirk D. GRIFFIN

Isaac Remembers

father carried the fire and knife
he spoke trembling with excuses
stacking wood on my back
i wondered if he understood the voice
or merely mouthed as he was told

the violence of his words took my breath
took my senses
took my love

did he worship the fire and knife and voice

a desperate bleating caught us both
then we knew the ram
would fall to blade and flame

and everything changed

after
we never spoke of it

because of the beast
i lived to inherit both knife and voice
i now understand them when they speak

know they are companion and teacher

only the fire is mine to make

Natural Beauty

i am always stunned
by the brightness of the sun
and by soft evenings
i drink the wind now
walking beneath ancient trees
trees that knew mankind
centuries before
i would ever touch
their massive shade or measure
their circumference
they are my touchstone
to a past i've only read
standing in this grove of green
i sense my smallness
and impermanence
wishing for roots, sun and rain
forever touching
the hand of God connecting
bold sky to sweet earth

Dirk D. GRIFFIN

Prière du Matin Pour les Morts[1]

my love of sin
dark, moonless
fills my nights

hear me o Lord
incline to me

even as my heart
sighs i bring myrrh
kiss your feet wet;
dry them clean with
my unworthy hair

hear me o Lord,
incline to me

you have gathered
the waters of the earth
bowed the heavens
bring now light to
my darkness

i know the fear
that gripped
Eve's heart
hearing your
footsteps echoing
in her sin

hear me o Lord
incline to me

know the shadows
in my soul
in the twilight
of paradise
bearing spices
to your tomb
knowing your judgments
will find the
depths of my sins

yet still i seek you
in love
still i seek you
in purity
i would be your handmaiden

hear me o Lord
incline to me
only your mercy
can be greater than
my fall

1   Morning Prayer For The Fallen

Dirk D. GRIFFIN

Shadows

after sundown doors hide in shadows
and shelter whores who ride the shadows

the moonlight aches to reach behind me
where lovers fight their pride in shadows

sweat and semen spill on silken beds
where couples seek comfort and shadows

my want, my need fails its concealment
without your touch i die in shadows

a raven flies beyond distant trees
and drops all silent into shadows

i prowl the streets; melt into shadows
where i live best at one with shadows

Come Spring

grey and wet
the world hangs
around me

still i marvel
at the colors
painting themselves
against that
backdrop

blooming loudly
flowers shout
against the overcast
darkened clouds

i am red
i am yellow
i am green
bright as the sun
shining
i renew

i renew

Dirk D. GRIFFIN

How To Save Yourself

sitting alone
moonless night
breathe a deep
blue breath

the world turns
with not for you
shiver night's
dark tendrils
snake over
skin

warm words
rush love's
memory spoken
kept
true

burn for other's
need of your
nearness

find
gather light reflected
from gentle eyes
caring

dusk
and dawn
are only passages
by which we
travel

it is not
the nature
of the world
to stop

Dirk D. GRIFFIN

Like Pollock

words fall on this page
crossing with meaning
and intent beyond
my poor reasoning

words fall on this page
like letters separate
purposeless without
caring what moment
they capture

words fall on this page
trees barren in a frozen
landscape stars fallen
from a cloudy sky

words fall
i mean
or perhaps
i don't

Night Cat

that
night
the cat
sang to me
in the dark alley
she unburdened her recent life
and only asked that
in return
i do
the
same

Dirk D. GRIFFIN

Sometimes Art

notebook in hand
the poet sat beside
a stream

two forms
eclipsed the sun

shadowed faces glared
are you the writer?

i'm the poet

are these your words?
growled the shades

the page unfurled
and was
read aloud

"and truth will keep you
warm in an honest embrace
sheltered from cold lies"

yes

the page was loosed
the poet caught it
the first blow fell

repeatedly
with boots
with fists
they pounded
silence from
the screams

they smashed
hands with rocks
threw water to wake
and began again

finally
bloody boot prints
in the notebook

DREAMING

"Never stop. Never stop fighting. Never stop dreaming."
~Tom Hiddleston~

Dirk D. GRIFFIN

Visit

time
runs
backwards
as i leaf
through these photographs;
faces, days, lost to memory
they are forever
black and white
smiling
their
youth

Sweet Swing

you can sashay swing to the rhythm fine.
you can sing, sing, sing and take the a train.
you can tap that beat from the jungle line.
can you cool this fever storming my brain?

maddening sounds are all about us now
i focus on you and the sugar push;
i focus on you, you become my tao:
you are sound, fury and a moment's hush.

behind your violet eyes flashing red,
between your breaths where eternity falls,
words of love are jazz'd and the things you've said
ride syncopations to break down my walls.

before you my life was empty of dance,
but your sweet swing brings me romance.

Dirk D. Griffin

Without

a cracked vessel alone
given to store
life

strained at every instance
breaking here or there
willed together with
glue and prayer

again a piece here falling
caught reclaimed
again bits lost within
and without

now stumble-fallen
crashed and spilled
beyond the glue
beyond the prayers
all these moments
this broken vessel

Ash

ash and smoke
and i

where fire
scourged and
leveled

a testimony of
impermanence
lingers

amid the wind
formless
and passing

becoming in part
part of
nothing

solid, liquid
vapor
becoming

ash and smoke
and i

Dirk D. GRIFFIN

Brandenburg Gate

Designer Genes

walking the helix
imagination released
seeking by instinct
a flow of ideas

ascending the ladder
carelessly floating
and recombining
unnaturally

building the unknown
from disparate pieces
a new age coming
from old now reformed

Dirk D. GRIFFIN

The Scrying Pool

dark water and candlelit
face reflecting bouncing light
the future answers my call

tomorrows crawl the surface
floating soft upon water
floating through my weak vision

this second sight a curse/gift
forcing me to witness things
i cannot understand

how can i speak what i've seen
how can i show what they mean
how can i know sage or fool
sybil of the scrying pool

A Dream of Happy Cows

dying from my life
i grabbed the white
hope a happy

pill
salt mixed with water
as i swallowed promised
relief into my system
dreaming i

became a happy cow
lolling through
affable meadows
blissful among the
other joyful jerseys
awaking i

became that blithe
beast lost among
others chemically
quieted by
that pharmaceutical

solace
my only value
sucked dry from my teats
excreted from my rectum
laughing to the end
of my

usefulness
i have seen the future

Dirk D. GRIFFIN

happy cows
sad cows
indifferent cows
angry cows

sacred cows

all dreams
scraped profanely
from my soul's corpse

i long to low in the moonlight
standing silent in the sun

River Ghosts

the river ghosts
guard the darkness
i see them keeping
watch about shores
in early light or new
twilight's haze

they speak fear
to weaker hearts

Dirk D. GRIFFIN

River Ghost

My Song

i thought i'd sing
a sweet refrain
a song to clear
the air

i thought i'd dance
some happiness
a soft shoe slide
to share

i thought someone
might notice and
their day would be
more fair

but no one smiled
all the while
face to the ground
they stare

i wonder
were they deaf?

held by shadows
beyond the sea
beyond you
beyond me

locked from desire
to love

to love or even
care

Dirk D. GRIFFIN

Fellini

i am fellini
in hidden dreams

burrowing into
the unconscious

elusive days dressed
in costumes,
skipping away

in my darkest dreams,
i am Fellini

Slaking

i'm drinking blue picassos in the rain,
wet with thoughts: newly baptized
amid this grey day i slip down to a crouch
that ghost floating above the canvas
is drenched in desire alone amid
hundreds of other shades walking through
the nude past the shadow drinking blue

Dirk D. GRIFFIN

Transformation

where the road
falls into the ocean

i look for some
sense at the beginning

silences breathe
stars fall

i become
sea and all

Dream Echoes

this dream echoes itself
night by night
i fly free on wings of light
throughout the stars
past moon and planets
comets of ice encased in fire
chase with me we dance afar
yet there is fear clutching my heart
as another stalks me among this heaven

it is a black wing
with hollow eyes
claws of fire
it rends the sky

seeking my heart
my joy
my sight
i tire of pursuit
turn to fight

too slow to counter
the claws' full slam
dilacerate both soul and man

then scattering my broken form
from system to system through
dust and storm

Dirk D. GRIFFIN

Stillborn

a raven at the cradle
the hammer falls to spark
i wish that i were able
to end this endless dark

a raven at the cradle
tomorrows die unknown
such blood upon my table
flows sorrows i have known

Vespers

cobblestones and dying
leaves at my feet
i walk this deserted courtyard
wind-blown among a rustle
scratching echoes
from the cracked plaster walls
painted orange-red
by the receding
sunset

Dirk D. GRIFFIN

Burning Faith

ice and snow without
the fire began within.
it licked the sacristy slowly
taking nourishment;
the aged wood gave
itself without struggle
to feed the growing
flame.

orange bright glow
suffused Saint Sebastian
before dissolving
him into molten
glass.

the flame moved
forward absorbing
relics remembrances
and rafters pushing
outward to walls
upward through ceiling
downward through floors
gathering strength with each
new convert
consumed.

men scurried on ladders
and with hoses tried to
staunch the destruction
but ice claimed the water
losing all to fire

Mersey[1] Beating

mercy
mersey beat sets my heart's pace
i jump and jive when i hear it flow
other sounds will come and go
but mersey beat is my rhythm's soul

mod
those modal tunes float through
my voice finds harmony too
blended with counter-melody
flats sharps notes of blue.

sounds
carry voices thought lost
we've moved on at cost
and i feel young inside this form
this odd language from other shores
a beat infused with electric vibes
mersey is a mercy in this old man's heart

---

[1] The Mersey Beat was a style of music made popular in the early to mid sixties by The Beatles and other Liverpool bands.

The Offer

shadows toy with my eyes
flicking darkness against
them again and again with
malice

consider the desolation
and the refuse that remains
strewn
fallen

all that is corrupt
all that is whole slammed
together in a bare
field of waste

come with me

please

come with me among
the remnants of this life
together we will sift

beauty from the ashes

Flash Photography

in that flash
i am twenty
then it subsides
white to
blue then
real

and i am me
wondering
how i can wear such
age when i
am so young

THE SACRED ARTS QUARTET

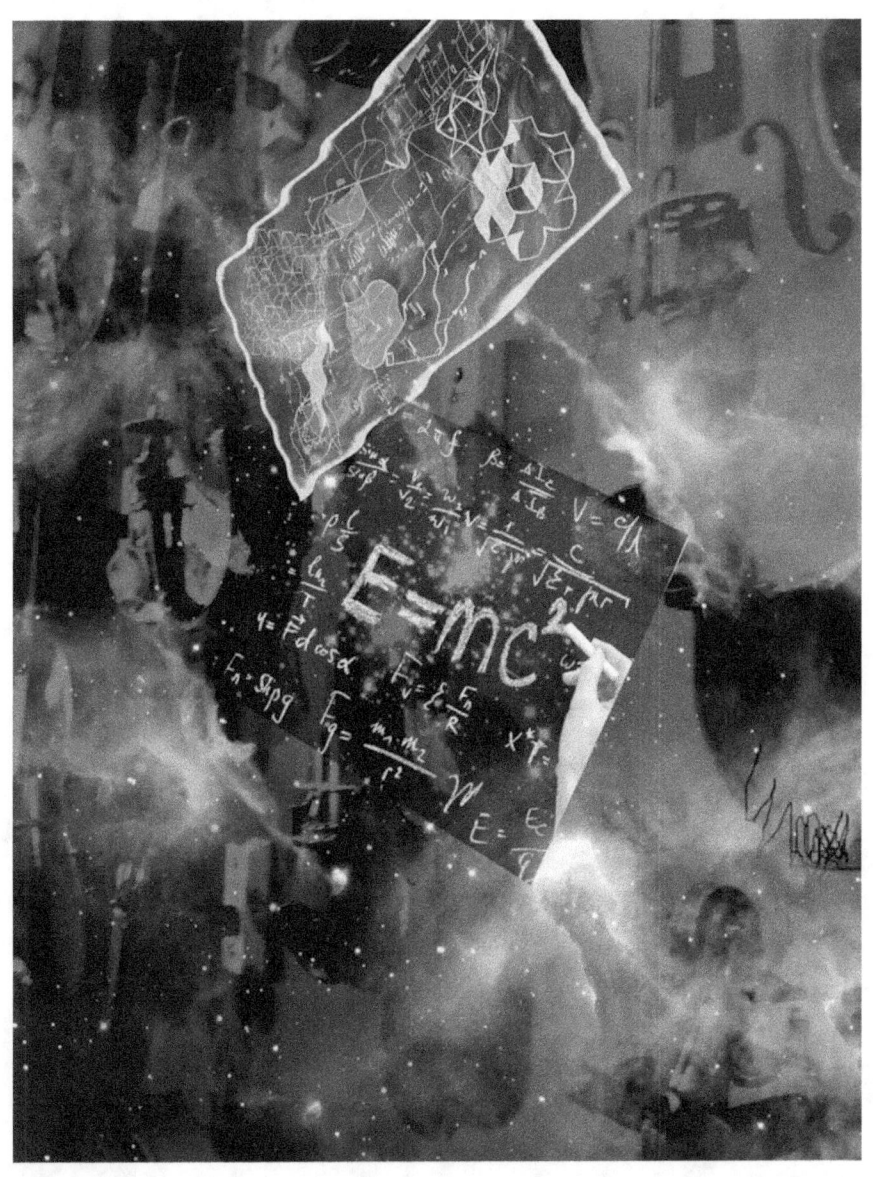

I. Geometry

begin with a point
expand to line
from there go
round the point
a line's distance
and from the point
from the line
the circle emerges

again
and again
circles proliferate
and lines
become polygons
become flowers
and expand beyond
to polyhedrons
of earth, air,
water, fire,
aether

a prayer of
being holy
of containing
and containment
from the one point
all proceeds

II. Music

flutes revered as
the voice of god
breathing loud
above the
pounding drums
rhythms jump and
crash against
bells in octaves ringing

quills
employed
to pluck or strum wires

voices
become prayers and find
the fourth above
rising and falling
triple meter
the voice of
ghosts in
practice

seeking David's
secret chord
the many who
raise voices and
strum, beat, pluck, shout
heaven's song

Dirk D. GRIFFIN

Floating Universe

III. Numbers

and so we kept count—
stones, days, people,
predators—
with marks and glyphs
etched in
rough stone
or soft clay

we sought
to quantify but
the I of one,
the V of five,
the L of
fifty restricted
us even as they
accounted
for all that
we had

still the sacred
numbers would not
flow until we
knew of nothing,
and zero brought
everything

it was
in knowing
nothing that

Dirk D. GRIFFIN

we could at last
count our way to dark
ocean depths, or
moons and planets far
with holy nothings
joined we reached
and touched the
silver stars

IV. Cosmology

in the beginning
we lay outstretched
beneath the deep
and glorious sky
and imagined a
wall between us
and some celestial
flame winking through
pin-pricks in that
untouchable domain

we traced fires
across its vast
territories;
naming lights,
telling tales,
following objects—
the debris of
infinity's birth—
and dreamed
of more

the constant sky
spoke through
generations,
empires,
gods and families
cloaking us
in eternity's
holy light

then
we touched the sky
stood upon
dry shores of
alien seas
and peered
into that distance
which swallows
understanding

among
the swirling
nebulae the
dust of worlds
destroyed
we knew ourselves
that we are beginning
and ending
that we are such
dust as sparks
to life throwing
questions into
the endless sky

ABOUT THE AUTHOR

Somewhere along the way, Dirk Griffin was bitten by the Renaissance Man bug. Among his many hats are singer/songwriter, composer, playwright, actor, photographer, digital artist, father, grandfather, technology whisperer, and general ne'er do well. Some of his music can be found at https://soundcloud.com/dirk-griffin. Additional writings can be found in various volumes of the Indian Creek Anthologies by the Southern Indiana Writers' Group http://southernindianawriters.com/?page_id=172. Artwork for home or clothing items are available at storefronts on http://ddgryphon.redbubble.com and http://www.zazzle.com/store/ddgryphon.

www.ingramcontent.com/pod-product-compliance
Lightning Source LLC
LaVergne TN
LVHW052341080426
835508LV00045B/3147